This is Blinker.

He is a little dog.

But what is the matter with him?

Look at his sad eyes!

Blinker is not happy.

Blinker has no home.

No one gives him food.

No one plays with him.

Poor Blinker is looking for a home.

He runs down the street.

He looks to the right

and he looks to the left.

He stops at every gate

and looks into every garden.

Is there no one

who wants a nice little dog?

Poor Blinker!
What have you done now?
The man gets angry
and gives Blinker a shower
from his watering can.

"Get off my flowers!
Get out of my garden!"
he shouts at Blinker.
And he gives Blinker
another shower of cold water.
Blinker is not very fond of water
and he thinks he had better
get out of the garden.
He takes another big jump –
and ... Poor Blinker!
He lands in another flower bed
with some very fine roses.

"My roses," cries the man.
Blinker is very, very quick
to leave the flower bed
and to leave the garden.

Blinker is sad again.
He is wet through
and the sharp thorns prick his nose.
That old man in the garden seems to care
more for flowers than for a little dog.
Blinker walks slowly
down the street.
Look at his tail
and his sad eyes!
It is not easy
to be a little dog
without a home.

"Honk! Honk!"

A big black car comes after him.

It looks terrible.

It has two big round eyes

and a big mouth with long teeth.

Blinker runs as fast as he can.

But the car runs after him.

At the end of the street

Blinker takes a sharp turn to the left.

The car turns to the right.

Blinker stops for a moment.

Look! The car is laughing at him!

The street is not a safe place
for a little dog.
Blinker thinks he had better
stay on the pavement.
But the pavement is full of legs,
a whole forest of legs
which are in a great hurry.
This place is no better.
Blinker is kicked and pushed.
No one has time
to care for a little dog.

Blinker runs and runs
away from the city,
away from the streets,
away from the busy people,
out into the country.
Now he is all alone
on a long, long road.
But he is not happy.
He has no home.
No one gives him food
and no one plays with him.

II

At the top of the hill
there is a little farm
with a white house and a red barn.
Blinker is tired and unhappy.
He can't run any longer.
He sits down on the roadside
and looks into the garden.
Maybe they want a little dog?
Just then a little red ball
comes rolling out of the garden
on to the road
and down into the ditch.

A boy comes out
and looks for the ball.
Where is it?
Blinker knows.

Maybe the boy is alone
and wants someone to play with?
Blinker jumps down into the ditch,
takes the ball in his mouth
and runs into the garden.
He puts the ball down
on the green grass.
He tries to look his best.
He wags his tail and
he looks at the boy with his
big brown eyes.

"What a nice little dog!"
says the boy and pats Blinker.
"Do you want to play with me?"
Of course Blinker wants to play!
He is happy!
And they play with the ball
the whole afternoon.
At last Blinker is tired.
The boy is tired, too.
They sit looking at each other.
Now farmer Brown comes back from the fields.
"Look Dad, what a nice little dog
I've found," says the boy.
"He has no home.
Can I keep him?"

"Of course you can keep him
if he has no home," says Bill's father.
"And if he is a nice dog," says
his mother.
Of course Blinker wants to be
a very nice dog!
At least he will do his best!

Now Blinker's eyes are sleepy.
Soon the boy and the dog are asleep
after this exciting day.
Sometimes Blinker's legs move ...
Maybe he is dreaming that the big
black car is hunting him
or that the busy feet in the street
are kicking him?
Or maybe he is dreaming
that he is playing with Bill?

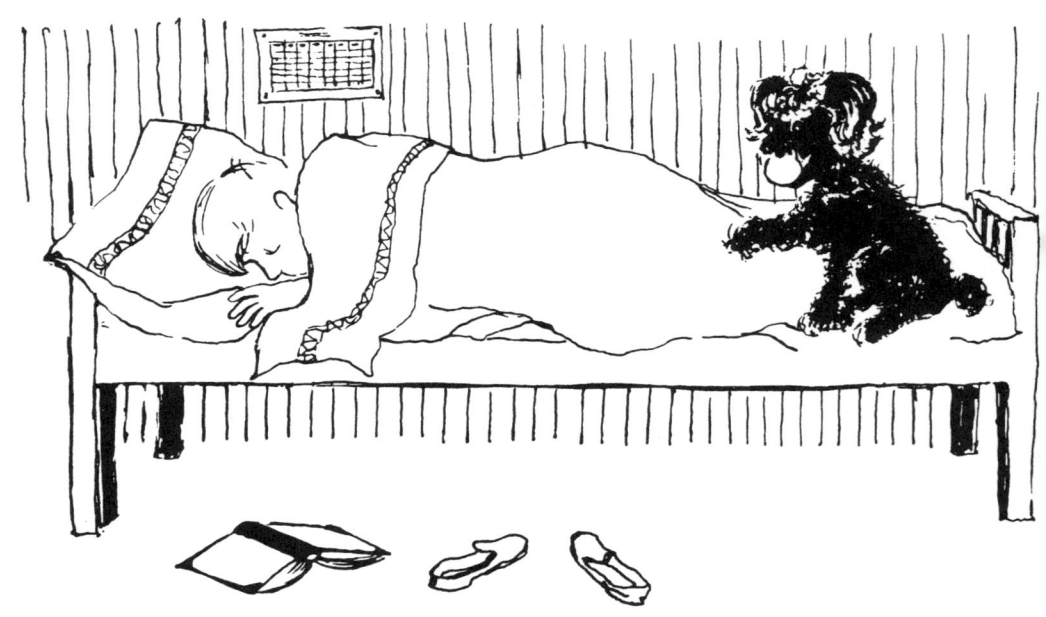

Next morning Blinker wakes up early.
Where is he?
He looks around.
No, there is no big car hunting him ...
And no busy feet are kicking him ...
There is a ball on the floor.
And there is a boy asleep in the bed.
Now Blinker remembers.
He takes the ball in his mouth
and jumps up on the bed.

16

But Bill has no time to play
with Blinker this morning.
He has to go to school.
Blinker will be alone
until Bill comes home.
"You stay here in the kitchen
and be a good dog, Blinker!"
Blinker lies down under the stove.
He takes the ball with him.
He will look after it.

But do you think
that a little dog
can lie quietly
under the stove
all day long?

Blinker simply *has to* be busy.
At least he wants to sit
outside the door and look ...
... for instance look at those
funny chickens, on the ground.
What will happen,
if he jumps in among them?
Look how they fly in all directions!
It is fun to chase them around.
Just for fun ...

But grown up people are strange.
Why are they not always friendly?
Why is Mrs. Brown so angry?
Blinker only wants to play
with the chickens.
He really will not hurt them.
He wants to run after them –
just for fun ...
Now he must stay in the kitchen
with a sign round his neck

saying
NAUGHTY DOG.
Look at
Blinker!

He wants to be
a good dog.

He had better lie down
under the stove again ...
Or at least stay in the kitchen ...
He can look through the window
if he jumps up on the chair ...
He will see even better
if he jumps up on the table ...
CRASH!
He has upset a vase of flowers.
Blinker thinks
he had better jump down
and go back to his place
under the stove.

Blinker is not very happy.
The sign round his neck says
NAUGHTY DOG.

Now he is quite sure
that something is wrong.
He had better lie down
under the stove again.
At once!
He just wants to see
what is behind that door ...

But what is this?
There is another dog!
Blinker has never seen
a mirror before.
And now he sees himself.

This other dog
looks so silly.
He has a sign
round his neck
with writing on it.

Blinker barks
at the other dog.
IMAGINE! THE DOG BARKS BACK!
Blinker gets angry.
He jumps up on the sideboard.
The other dog jumps, too.
There he is ...
Go away, or ...
There is a terrible fight.
Crash! Crash!
Where is the other dog?
He has gone.
Blinker has won the fight.

But he is not quite sure
that everything is alright ...
Now Blinker has to get back
to his place in the kitchen.
He had better stay there
until Bill comes home.

Mrs. Brown comes in.
She has heard the noise.
"Who has done all this?
You, Blinker?"
Blinker can't understand
why she is angry.
"Why can't you be
a good dog?"
Of course Blinker wants
to be a good dog.

Just look at him!
Can you imagine
that Blinker wants to break a vase
or upset a bowl
or break a mirror?
At last Bill comes home from school.
"Look what your dog has done!"
says Mrs. Brown.

Bill and Blinker look at each other.
"Poor Blinker! Come here!
I'll take the sign away.
Of course you don't know
how to behave in a house.
You've never had a home.
But you'll learn."
Blinker is happy again.
He wags his tail.

This is Bill's last day of school.
The long summer holidays
lie before Bill and Blinker
with happy days of play and fun.

Blinker tries to be nice dog.
And he *is* a nice dog.
Of course he sometimes
hunts the chickens
or upsets the milk bottles
or treads on the good carpet
with his dirty feet
or breaks a plate
or treads on the flower beds ...
But he never *intends* to do so.

One day there is a letter for Bill.
It is from Uncle Martin.
He asks Bill to come and visit him
for a week or so.
Uncle Martin has a small factory
near a big lake.
Bill is happy.
But Blinker is sad
because he will be
left at home.

Next morning Bill gets up early
because he has to catch an early train.
He puts his things into a case:
toothbrush and toothpaste,
slippers, pyjamas, an extra shirt,
and swimming trunks.
Bill hurries down to eat his breakfast.
He leaves the case open.

Blinker wonders what is in it.
He gets hold of the pyjamas
and drags them away under the bed.
And the toothbrush, too,
and the shirt.

29

Then he takes the ball
and jumps up into the case
and tastes the toothpaste.
BANG!
The lid falls down and Blinker is trapped.
Bill is in a hurry.
He takes his case and runs.

There comes the train!
It takes Bill to his uncle.
Is there no one to meet him?
Bill takes his case and walks.
How heavy the case is!
Bill has to sit and rest.

But there comes Uncle Martin!
And he helps Bill with the case.
"What have you got in your case?
It's so heavy."
"My pyjamas, my toothbrush and toothpaste,
my slippers, and an extra shirt."
"Maybe it's the extra shirt that's so heavy,"
says Uncle Martin and laughs.

Imagine Bill's surprise
when he opens the case!
There is Blinker and the ball
but no pyjamas
and no shirt
and no toothbrush
and no slippers.

That night Bill has to wear
Uncle Martin's big pyjamas.
He looks very funny.
Uncle Martin laughs at him.
Even Blinker seems
to have fun.
"You naughty dog,"
says Bill.
But he can't
be angry with him.

Bill and Blinker have a lot of fun.
They play on the beach
and sail in Uncle Martin's boat.
One day Bill sees
Uncle Martin's little factory
where they make electric bells.
Blinker stays outside
because he is afraid
of the rattling machines.
Soon he finds something
interesting to look at.
It looks like a ball.
But it is a hedgehog.
Blinker has never seen a hedgehog before
and he pricks his nose
when he tries to play with it.

Then one day it happens:
the great event that makes Blinker FAMOUS.
Bill and Blinker are out sailing.
A sudden wind overturns the boat
and they both fall into the water.
Bill can't swim all the way to the shore.
He will drown unless he gets help.
Blinker fights against the water.
He swims as fast as he can
and he reaches the shore.
Then he runs to the factory.
He even dares to go into the factory
with all its rattling machines.

Uncle Martin understands
that something must be wrong.
He follows Blinker down to the shore.
There is Bill, fighting for his life.
Uncle Martin reaches Bill just in time
to save him.
Blinker is tired but happy.
When Bill feels better
he can't find words
to thank Uncle and to thank Blinker.
Next day Uncle Martin drives Bill
and Blinker back to Bill's home.

And he tells Bill's parents
how brave Blinker was.
Of course they are happy.
They are proud that Blinker is THEIR dog.
"You're a wonderful dog, Blinker!
We won't call you
NAUGHTY DOG
anymore.

We'll make you wear
a new sign that says
GOOD BLINKER."

Uncle Martin takes a picture
of Bill and Blinker.

They all drive into town
and tell Blinker's story to the
newspaper reporter.

Soon his photo hangs in the
window. People who pass by
stop and look and read:
"A LITTLE DOG SAVES A BOY."
And the man in the garden
with the pretty flowers opens
his newspaper and reads:
"A LITTLE DOG SAVES A BOY."

This is a happy day for Blinker.
He beams with pride.
And Bill hangs a picture of Blinker
over his bed.
Here it is.

Wörterverzeichnis nach Seiten

3

little klein
dog Hund
but (bʌt) aber
What is the matter with him?
  Was ist mit ihm los?
to look (lʊk) schauen, aussehen;
  Look! Schau!
sad (sæd) traurig
eye (aɪ) Auge

4/5

He has no home. Er hat kein Zuhause.
no one (ˈnəʊwʌn) niemand
food (fuːd) Futter, Fressen
to play (pleɪ) spielen
with (wɪð) mit
poor (pɔː) arm
to look for suchen (nach)
to run (rʌn) rennen
down (daʊn) hinunter
street (striːt) Straße
to look to the right (raɪt) nach rechts
  gucken
to the left nach links
every jede, jeder, jedes
gate (geɪt) Gartentor, Pforte
Is there no one who ...? Gibt es keinen,
  der ...?
to want (wɒnt) wollen
nice (naɪs) nett, lieb
lovely schön
lots of (ˈlɒtsəv) viele
pretty (ˈprɪtɪ) hübsch, schön
flower (ˈflaʊə) Blume
open (ˈəʊpən) offen
there (ðeə) da, dort

old (əʊld) alt
to water (ˈwɔːtə) gießen
maybe (ˈmeɪbɪ) vielleicht

6/7

to try (traɪ) versuchen; **he/she tries**
  (traɪz) er/sie versucht
to look his best bestmöglich aussehen
He wags his tail. (wægz; teɪl)
  Er wedelt mit seinem Schwanz.
He pricks up his ears. (ɪəz) Er spitzt
  seine Ohren.
big groß
to have no time keine Zeit haben
to take a jump (dʒʌmp) einen Sprung
  machen
among (əˈmʌŋ) zwischen, inmitten
What have you done now? (dʌn; naʊ)
  Was hast du jetzt gemacht?
angry (ˈæŋgrɪ) wütend
shower (ˈʃaʊə) Dusche
watering can (ˈwɔːtərɪŋkæn) Gießkanne
Get off my flowers! Geh weg von meinen
  Blumen! Komm aus meinem Blumenbeet heraus!
Get out of my garden! Verschwinde aus
  meinem Garten! Raus aus meinem
  Garten! **to get out** verschwinden,
  hinauskommen
to shout at someone (ʃaʊt) jemanden
  anbrüllen, -schreien
to be fond of something (fɒnd) etwas
  mögen
to think (θɪŋk) denken
he had better ... er wäre besser ...
another (əˈnʌðə) noch einer, -eine, -eines
flower bed Blumenbeet
very (ˈverɪ) sehr

8/9

to **cry** (kraɪ) rufen; **he/she cries** (kraɪz) er/sie ruft

quick schnell

to **leave** (liːv) verlassen

again (əˈgen) wieder, erneut

to **be wet through** (θruː) durchnässt sein

sharp spitz, scharf

thorn (θɔːn) Dorn

to **prick** stechen, pieksen

to **seem** (siːm) scheinen, den Anschein erwecken

to **care for something** (keə) etwas mögen

than (ðæn) als

to **walk** (wɔːk) gehen

slowly (ˈsləʊlɪ) langsam

easy (ˈiːzɪ) leicht

without (wɪˈðaʊt) ohne

Honk! Tut! (**to honk** hupen)

to **come after someone** jemanden verfolgen

terrible (ˈterəbl) schrecklich, furchtbar

mouth (maʊθ) Mund, Maul, Schnauze

teeth (tiːθ) Zähne

fast (fɑːst) schnell

to **take a sharp turn to the left** (tɜːn) scharf nach links abbiegen; to **turn to the right** nach rechts abbiegen

to **laugh at someone** (lɑːf) jemanden auslachen; to **laugh** lachen

10/11

safe sicher

place Ort

to **stay** (steɪ) bleiben, sich aufhalten

pavement (ˈpeɪvmənt) Bürgersteig, Gehweg

leg Bein

whole (həʊl) ganz

forest (ˈfɒrɪst) Wald

to **be in a great hurry** (ˈhʌrɪ) es sehr eilig haben; to **hurry** eilen

to **kick** mit den Füßen treten

to **push** (pʊʃ) stoßen, schubsen

to **care for** sich kümmern um

busy (ˈbɪzɪ) geschäftig, (Straße) verkehrsreich

people (ˈpiːpl) Leute, Menschen

out into the country (ˈkʌntrɪ) raus aufs Land

road Straße

happy glücklich

12/13

at the top of the hill oben auf dem Hügel

barn Scheune

tired (ˈtaɪəd) müde

unhappy (ʌnˈhæpɪ) unglücklich

he can't er kann nicht

not any longer nicht länger, nicht mehr

just then (dʒʌst; ðen) genau-, ausgerechnet dann

ditch (dɪtʃ) Straßengraben

boy Junge

to **know** (nəʊ) (es) wissen

to **jump down** hinunterspringen

to **put down** ablegen

14/15

to **pat** (pæt) tätscheln, einen freundlichen Klaps geben

39

of course (əv'kɔ:s) natürlich
afternoon (ˌɑːftə'nuːn) Nachmittag
at last letztendlich, am Ende, endlich
They look at each other. (ˌiːtʃ'ʌðə)
    Sie gucken sich gegenseitig an.
back zurück
Dad Vati, Papa
I've/I have (aɪv) ich habe
to find (faɪnd) finden; found (faʊnd)
    gefunden
to keep (kiːp) behalten
if wenn, falls
at least (liːst) zumindest, wenigstens
sleepy ('sliːpɪ) schläfrig
to be asleep (ə'sliːp) schlafen
exciting (ɪk'saɪtɪŋ) aufregend
sometimes ('sʌmtaɪmz) manchmal
to move (muːv) sich bewegen
to dream (driːm) träumen
to hunt (hʌnt) jagen
feet (fiːt) Füße; foot (fʊt) Fuß

16/17
to wake up (weɪk) aufwachen
early ('ɜːlɪ) früh
Where is he? Wo ist er?
to look around sich umsehen
floor (flɔː) Fußboden
to remember (rɪ'membə) sich erinnern
to jump up aufspringen
to have to go gehen müssen
school (skuːl) Schule
until (ʌn'tɪl) bis
kitchen ('kɪtʃɪn) Küche
good gut, brav
to lie down (laɪ) sich hinlegen

stove (stəʊv) Ofen, Herd
to look after something auf etwas
    aufpassen
quietly ('kwaɪətlɪ) ruhig
all day long den ganzen Tag

18/19
simply einfach
for instance ('ɪnstəns) zum Beispiel
funny ('fʌnɪ) witzig, seltsam
chicken ('tʃɪkɪn) Huhn
on the ground auf dem Boden
What will happen? ('hæpən) Was wird
    passieren?
to fly (flaɪ) fliegen
direction (dɪ'rekʃən) Richtung
to be fun Spaß machen; just for fun nur
    zum Spaß
to chase around (tʃeɪs) umherjagen
grown up people ('grəʊnʌp) Erwachsene
strange (streɪndʒ) seltsam, sonderbar
always ('ɔːlweɪz) immer
friendly ('frendlɪ) freundlich
only ('əʊnlɪ) nur
really ('rɪəlɪ) wirklich
to hurt someone (hɜːt) jemandem
    wehtun
sign (saɪn) Schild
round um
neck Hals
saying ... ('seɪɪŋ) auf dem ... steht
    (to say sagen)
naughty ('nɔːtɪ) ungezogen, unartig

20/21

window ('wɪndəʊ) Fenster
chair (tʃeə) Stuhl
even ('iːvən) noch
table ('teɪbl) Tisch
to upset (ʌp'set) umwerfen
vase (vɑːz) Vase
to be afraid (ə'freɪd) Angst haben,
befürchten
something is wrong (rɒŋ) etwas stimmt
nicht
fly (flaɪ) Fliege
to annoy (ə'nɔɪ) ärgern, nerven
to buzz (bʌz) schwirren, summen
Go away! (ə'weɪ) Weg mit dir!, Geh weg!
or I will ... oder ich werde ...
to snap at (snæp) schnappen nach

22/23

to sit sitzen
bowl (bəʊl) Schüssel, Schale
milk Milch
paw (pɔː) Pfote
Can he help it? Kann er etwas dafür?
anyhow ('enɪhaʊ) trotzdem, dennoch
to be ashamed (ə'ʃeɪmd) sich schämen
quite (kwaɪt) ziemlich; ganz
sure (ʃʊə) sicher
at once (wʌns) sofort
just (dʒʌst) nur
behind (bɪ'haɪnd) hinter
mirror ('mɪrə) Spiegel
himself sich selbst
silly albern, doof
writing Schrift

24/25

to bark bellen, kläffen
to imagine (ɪ'mædʒɪn) sich vorstellen;
Imagine! Stell dir vor!
sideboard hier: Spiegelkommode
too auch
fight (faɪt) Kampf
he has gone (ɡɒn) er ist fort
to win gewinnen; **won** (wʌn) gewonnen
alright (ɔːl'raɪ) in Ordnung
he has to er muss
to get back zurückgehen
to hear (hɪə) hören; **heard** (hɜːd) gehört
noise (nɔɪz) Lärm
Who has done all this? Wer hat all das
getan?
to understand verstehen
to break (breːk) zerbrechen, kaputtmachen

26/27

I'll/I will ... ich werde ...
don't = do not
to behave (bɪ'heɪv) sich verhalten, sich
benehmen
You've never had a home. Du hattest
noch nie ein Zuhause.
you'll/you will learn (lɜːn) du wirst
(das) lernen
last letzte, letzter, letztes
summer holidays ('hɒlədeɪz) Sommer-
ferien
to lie before someone (laɪ) vor jemandem liegen
to tread on (tred) betreten, treten auf
carpet ('kɑːpɪt) Teppich

dirty ('dɜːtɪ) schmutzig
plate (pleɪt) Teller
to intend (ɪn'tend) beabsichtigen, wollen

28/29

letter Brief
uncle ('ʌŋkl) Onkel
to ask einladen, bitten
to visit besuchen
small (smɔːl) klein
factory ('fæktərɪ) Fabrik
near (nɪə) in der Nähe von
lake (leɪk) See
because ('bɪkɔz) weil
to leave (liːv) zurücklassen; left zurückgelassen
next morning am nächsten Morgen
to get up aufstehen
early ('ɜːlɪ) früh
to catch a train (treɪn) einen Zug
nehmen
to put legen, stecken
case Koffer
toothbrush ('tuːθbrʌʃ) Zahnbürste
toothpaste ('tuːθpeɪst) Zahnpasta
slippers Hausschuhe
pyjamas (pɪ'dʒɑːməz) Schlafanzug
swimming trunks ('swɪmɪŋ,trʌŋks)
Badehose
to hurry down ('hʌrɪ) schnell hinunter-
gehen
to eat (iːt) essen
breakfast ('brekfəst) Frühstück
to leave lassen
to wonder ('wʌndə) sich fragen

to get hold of something (həʊld) etwas
erwischen, - packen
to drag away wegziehen, wegschleifen

30/31

to taste (teɪst) probieren
lid Deckel
to be trapped (træpt) gefangen sein
to be in a hurry es eilig haben
to take nehmen; bringen
to meet (miːt) treffen, hier: abholen
heavy ('hevɪ) schwer
to rest sich ausruhen, eine Pause machen
surprise (sə'praɪz) Überraschung
to wear (weə) tragen
funny lustig

32/33

on the beach am Strand
to sail (seɪl) segeln
electric bell (ɪ'lektrɪk) elektrische Klingel
outside (,aʊt'saɪd) draußen
rattling ('rætlɪŋ) klappernd, scheppernd,
rasselnd
hedgehog ('hedʒhɒg) Igel
he has never seen a ... er hat noch nie
einen ... gesehen
he pricks his nose seine Nase wird
gepiekst; - gestochen
great (greɪt) groß
event (ɪ'vent) Ereignis, Vorfall
famous ('feɪməs) berühmt
sudden ('sʌdən) plötzlich
to overturn (,əʊvə'tɜːn) umstoßen,
kentern lassen
shore (ʃɔː) Küste, Ufer
to drown (draʊn) ertrinken

unless (ən'les) es sei denn
help Hilfe
to fight against something (faɪt) gegen
etwas kämpfen
to reach (riːtʃ) erreichen
even ('iːvən) sogar
to dare to do (deə) sich trauen zu tun

34/35
to follow ('fɒləʊ) folgen
he is fighting for his life er kämpft um
sein Leben
just in time gerade noch rechtzeitig
to save (seɪv) retten
to feel better sich besser fühlen
to thank (θæŋk) danken
to drive (draɪv) fahren
to tell erzählen
parents ('peərənts) Eltern
brave (breɪv) mutig
proud (praʊd) stolz
wonderful ('wʌndəfəl) wunderbar
we won't/we will not wir werden nicht
to call (kɔːl) nennen

36/37
to take a picture ('pɪktʃə) ein Foto
machen
town (taʊn) Stadt
newspaper reporter ('njuːsˌpeɪpə; rɪ'pɔːtə)
Journalist
to pass by vorbeigehen
to read (riːd) lesen
soon (suːn) bald
to beam with pride (biːm; praɪd) vor
Stolz strahlen

Alphabetisches Wörterverzeichnis

A

(to be) afraid (əˈfreɪd) Angst haben, befürchten
after nach, hinter
afternoon (ˌɑːftəˈnuːn) Nachmittag
again (əˈgen) wieder, erneut
against (əˈgenst) gegen
all the way den ganzen Weg
alone allein
alright (ɔːlˈraɪt) in Ordnung
also (ˈɔːlsəʊ) auch, ebenfalls
always (ˈɔːlweɪz) immer
among (əˈmʌŋ) zwischen, inmitten
angry (ˈæŋgrɪ) wütend
(to) annoy (əˈnɔɪ) ärgern, nerven
another (əˈnʌðə) noch einer, -eine, -eines
not any longer nicht länger, nicht mehr
anyhow (ˈenɪhaʊ) trotzdem, dennoch
as ... as so ... wie
(to be) ashamed (əˈʃeɪmd) sich schämen
(to) ask einladen, bitten
at last (lɑːst) letztendlich, am Ende, endlich
at least (liːst) zumindest, wenigstens
(to be) asleep (əˈsliːp) schlafen
away (əˈweɪ) weg

B

back zurück
(to) bark bellen, kläffen
(to) bark at anbellen
barn Scheune
(to) be sein
(to) beam with pride (biːm; praɪd) vor Stolz strahlen
because (bɪˈkɔz) weil

bed Bett
before vor, vorher
(to) behave (bɪˈheɪv) sich verhalten, sich benehmen
behind (bɪˈhaɪnd) hinter
bell Klingel
he had better ... er wäre besser ..., er hätte besser ...
big groß
black schwarz
boat Boot
both (bəʊθ) beide
bowl (bəʊl) Schüssel, Schale
boy Junge
brave (breɪv) mutig
(to) break (breɪk) zerbrechen, kaputtmachen
breakfast (ˈbrekfəst) Frühstück
brown (braʊn) braun
busy (ˈbɪzɪ) geschäftig, (Straße) verkehrsreich
but aber
(to) buzz (bʌz) schwirren, summen

C

(to) call (kɔːl) nennen
he can er kann; **we can** wir können
he/she/it can't/cannot er/sie/es kann nicht
car Auto
(to) care for something (keə) etwas mögen;
  (to) care for sich kümmern um
carpet (ˈkɑːpɪt) Teppich
chair (tʃeə) Stuhl
(to) chase around (tʃeɪs) umherjagen
chicken (ˈtʃɪkɪn) Huhn
cold kalt
(to) come after someone jemanden verfolgen
country (ˈkʌntrɪ) Land

of course (əv'kɔːs) natürlich
(to) cry (kraı) rufen; he/she cries (kraız) er/sie ruft

D

Dad Vati, Papa
(to) dare to do (deə) sich trauen zu tun
day Tag
direction (dı'rekʃən) Richtung
dirty ('dɜːtı) schmutzig
ditch (dıtʃ) Straßengraben
(to) do tun; done (dʌn) getan
dog Hund
door Tür
down (daʊn) hinunter
(to) drag away wegziehen, wegschleifen
(to) dream (driːm) träumen
(to) drive (draıv) fahren
(to) drown (draʊn) ertrinken

E

each other (ˌiːtʃˈʌðə) einander, gegenseitig
ear (ıə) Ohr
early ('ɜːlı) früh
easy ('iːzı) leicht
(to) eat (iːt) essen
electric (ı'lektrık) elektrisch
enough (ı'nʌf) genug
even ('iːvən) sogar; noch
event (ı'vent) Ereignis, Vorfall
every jeder, jede, jedes
everything ('evrıθıŋ) alles
exciting (ık'saıtıŋ) aufregend
eye (aı) Auge

F

factory ('fæktərı) Fabrik
(to) fall fallen
famous ('feıməs) berühmt
farm Bauernhof
farmer Bauer
fast (faːst) schnell
father ('faːðə) Vater
(to) feel (fiːl) sich fühlen
feet (fiːt) Füße; foot (fʊt) Fuß
field Feld, Acker
fight (faıt) Kampf; (to) fight kämpfen
(to) find (faınd) finden; found (faʊnd) gefunden
fine (faın) herrlich, schön
floor (flɔː) Fußboden
flower ('flaʊə) Blume
flowerbed Blumenbeet
(to) fly (flaı) fliegen
fly (flaı) Fliege
(to) follow ('fɒləʊ) folgen
(to be) fond of something (fɒnd) etwas mögen, -gern haben
food (fuːd) Futter, Fressen, Nahrung
forest ('fɒrıst) Wald
friendly ('frendlı) freundlich
from von, aus
fun Spaß; to be fun Spaß machen; just for fun nur zum Spaß
funny ('fʌnı) witzig, seltsam

G

garden Garten
gate (geıt) Gartentor, Pforte
(to) get bekommen, werden; got bekam, bekommen; What have you got ...? Was hast du ...?

to go away weggehen
to get back zurückkommen
to get off verlassen, herauskommen
to get out verschwinden, hinauskommen
to get up aufstehen
(to) give geben
(to) go gehen, fahren; he is to go er soll
  fahren
good gut; brav
grass Gras
great (greɪt) groß
green grün
on the ground auf dem Boden, auf der
  Erde
grown up ('grəʊnʌp) erwachsen

H

(to) hang hängen, aufhängen
(to) happen ('hæpən) passieren
happy glücklich
(to) have haben; (to) have to do tun
  müssen
(to) hear (hɪə) hören; heard (hɜːd)
  gehört
heavy ('hevɪ) schwer
hedgehog ('hedʒhɒg) Igel
help Hilfe; Can he help it? Kann er
  etwas dafür?
here hier
hill Hügel
himself sich selbst
to get hold of something (həʊld) etwas
  erwischen, – packen
holidays ('hɒlədeɪz) Ferien
home Zuhause
(to) honk hupen; Honk! Tut!
house Haus

how (haʊ) wie
(to) hunt (hʌnt) jagen
hurry ('hʌrɪ) Eile; to be in a great hurry
  es sehr eilig haben; to hurry eilen
(to) hurt someone (hɜːt) jemandem
  wehtun

I

if wenn, falls
(to) imagine (ɪ'mædʒɪn) sich vorstellen;
  Imagine! Stell dir vor!
for instance ('ɪnstəns) zum Beispiel
(to) intend (ɪn'tend) beabsichtigen,
  wollen
interesting ('ɪntrəstɪŋ) interessant
into hinein in

J

to take a jump (dʒʌmp) einen Sprung
  machen; (to) jump springen;
  to jump down hinunterspringen;
  to jump up aufspringen
just (dʒʌst) gerade, nur, genau

K

(to) keep (kiːp) behalten
kitchen ('kɪtʃɪn) Küche
(to) know (nəʊ) (es) wissen

L

lake (leɪk) See
(to) land landen
last (lɑːst) letzter, letzte, letztes
at last letztendlich, am Ende, endlich

(to) laugh (lɑːf) lachen; **(to) laugh at someone** jemanden auslachen
(to) learn (lɜːn) lernen
at least (liːst) zumindest, wenigstens
(to) leave (liːv) lassen, zurücklassen, verlassen; **left** zurückgelassen
left links
to the left nach links
leg Bein
letter Brief
lid Deckel
(to) lie down (laɪ) sich hinlegen; **to lie before someone** vor jemandem liegen
life Leben
like wie
little klein
long lang, lange
(to) look (lʊk) schauen, aussehen; **Look!** Schau!
(to) look after something auf etwas aufpassen
(to) look around sich umsehen
(to) look for suchen (nach), sich umsehen nach
(to) look at ansehen
lots of (ˈlɔtsəv) viele
lovely schön

M

machine (məˈʃiːn) Maschine
(to) make machen
man Mann
What is the matter? Was ist los?
maybe (ˈmeɪbɪ) vielleicht
(to) meet (miːt) treffen, hier: abholen
milk Milch; **milk bottle** Milchflasche
mirror (ˈmɪrə) Spiegel

moment (ˈməʊmənt) Augenblick, Moment
more mehr
morning Morgen
mother (ˈmʌðə) Mutter
mouth (maʊθ) Mund, Maul, Schnauze
(to) move (muːv) (sich) bewegen
must muss

N

naughty (ˈnɔːtɪ) ungezogen, unartig
near (nɪə) in der Nähe von
neck Hals
never niemals, noch nie
new (njuː) neu
newspaper reporter (ˈnjuːsˌpeɪpə; rɪˈpɔːtə) Journalist
next nächster, nächste, nächstes
nice (naɪs) nett, lieb
night (naɪt) Nacht
no nein, kein
no one (ˈnəʊwʌn) niemand
noise (nɔɪz) Lärm
nose (nəʊz) Nase
not nicht
now (naʊ) jetzt

O

of von
off weg, davon
old (əʊld) alt
on auf
at once (wʌns) sofort
one ein; **one day** eines Tages
only (ˈəʊnlɪ) nur
open (ˈəʊpə) offen
or oder
other (ˈʌðə) anderer, andere, anderes

out aus, heraus, hinaus
outside (ˌaʊtˈsaɪd) draußen
over über
(to) overturn (ˌəʊvəˈtɜːn) umstoßen,
kentern lassen

P

parents (ˈpeərənts) Eltern
(to) pat (pæt) tätscheln, einen freundlichen Klaps geben
pavement (ˈpeɪvmənt) Bürgersteig,
Gehweg
paw (pɔː) Pfote
to pass by (paːs) vorbeigehen
people (ˈpiːpl) Leute
picture (ˈpɪktʃə) Foto, Bild
place Ort
plate (pleɪt) Teller
(to) play spielen
poor (pɔː) arm
pretty (ˈprɪtɪ) hübsch, schön
(to) prick stechen, pieksen; **he pricks
up his ears** (ɪəz) er spitzt seine Ohren
pride (praɪd) Stolz
proud (praʊd) stolz
(to) push (pʊʃ) stoßen, schubsen,
schieben
(to) put (pʊt) legen, stecken; **(to) put
down** ablegen
pyjamas (pɪˈdʒɑːməz) Schlafanzug

Q

quick schnell
quiet (ˈkwaɪət) ruhig
quite (kwaɪt) ganz, ziemlich

R

rattling (ˈrætlɪŋ) klappernd, scheppernd,
rasselnd
(to) reach (riːtʃ) erreichen, herankom-
men an
(to) read (riːd) lesen
really (ˈrɪəlɪ) wirklich
red rot
(to) remember (rɪˈmembə) sich erinnern
(to) rest sich ausruhen, eine Pause
machen
right (raɪt) rechts
to the right nach rechts
road Straße
on the roadside am Straßenrand
(to) roll (rəʊl) rollen
rose (rəʊz) Rose
round um, rund herum
(to) run (rʌn) rennen

S

sad (sæd) traurig
safe (seɪf) sicher
(to) sail (seɪl) segeln
(to) save (seɪv) retten
(to) say sagen; **saying ...** (ˈseɪɪŋ) auf dem
... steht
school (skuːl) Schule
(to) see sehen
(to) seem (siːm) scheinen, den Anschein
erwecken
sharp spitz, scharf
shore (ʃɔː) Küste, Strand, Ufer
(to) shout at someone (ʃaʊt) jemanden
anschreien, - brüllen
shower (ˈʃaʊə) Dusche
sideboard hier: Spiegelkommode

sign (saɪn) Schild
silly albern, doof
simply einfach
(to) sit sitzen
(to) sleep (sliːp) schlafen
sleepy ('sliːpɪ) schläfrig
slippers Hausschuhe
slowly ('sləʊlɪ) langsam
small (smɔːl) klein
(to) snap at (snæp) schnappen nach
something ('sʌmθɪŋ) etwas
sometimes ('sʌmtaɪmz) manchmal
soon (suːn) bald
(to) stay (steɪ) bleiben, sich aufhalten
still noch
stove (stəʊv) Ofen, Herd
strange seltsam, sonderbar
street (striːt) Straße
sudden ('sʌdən) plötzlich
summer Sommer
sure (ʃʊə) sicher
surprise (sə'praɪz) Überraschung
(to) swim schwimmen
swimming trunks ('swɪmɪŋˌtrʌŋks)
    Badehose

T

table ('teɪbl) Tisch
tail (teɪl) Schwanz
(to) take nehmen
to take a picture ein Foto machen
(to) taste (teɪst) probieren
teeth (tiːθ) Zähne
(to) tell erzählen
terrible ('terəbl) schrecklich, furchtbar
than (ðæn) als
(to) thank (θæŋk) danken
that dass; dies(er)

then (ðen) dann
there (ðeə) da, dort
thing Ding, Sache
(to) think (θɪŋk) denken
this diese, dieser, dieses
thorn (θɔːn) Dorn
those (ðəʊz) jene, diese
through (θruː) durch und durch
time Zeit; to have no time keine Zeit
    haben
just in time gerade noch rechtzeitig
tired ('taɪəd) müde
to bis, nach, zu
too (tuː) auch
toothbrush ('tuːθbrʌʃ) Zahnbürste
toothpaste ('tuːθpeɪst) Zahnpasta
top Gipfel, oberes Ende, Spitze; at the
    top of the hill oben auf dem Hügel
town (taʊn) Stadt
train (treɪn) Zug
(to be) trapped (træpt) gefangen sein
(to) tread on (tred) betreten, treten auf
(to) try (traɪ) versuchen; he/she tries
    (traɪz) er/sie versucht
turn (tɜːn) Wendung, Drehung
(to) turn abbiegen
two (tuː) zwei

U

uncle ('ʌŋkl) Onkel
under unter
(to) understand (ˌʌndə'stænd) verstehen
unhappy (ʌn'hæpɪ) unglücklich
unless (ən'les) es sei denn
until (ʌn'tɪl) bis
up auf, hinauf
(to) upset (ʌp'set) umwerfen

V

vase (vɑːz) Vase
very ('verɪ) sehr
(to) visit besuchen

W

(to) wake up (weɪk) aufwachen
(to) walk (wɔːk) gehen
(to) want (wɒnt) wollen, wünschen
(to) water ('wɔːtə) gießen
watering can ('wɔːtərɪŋkæn) Gießkanne
way (weɪ) Weg
(to) wear (weə) tragen
week (wiːk) Woche
wet nass; to be wet through durchnässt
  sein
what was
when als
where wo
which (wɪtʃ) welcher, welche, welches

white weiß
who (huː) wer
whole (həʊl) ganz
why wieso, warum
(to) wag (wæg) wedeln
(to) win gewinnen;
  won (wʌn) gewonnen
wind Wind
window ('wɪndəʊ) Fenster
will werde, wirst, wird, werden, werdet;
  I will/I'll ich werde
with (wɪð) mit
without (wɪˈðaʊt) ohne
(to) wonder ('wʌndə) sich fragen
word Wort
writing ('raɪtɪŋ) Schrift
wrong (rɒŋ) falsch; something is
  wrong etwas stimmt nicht

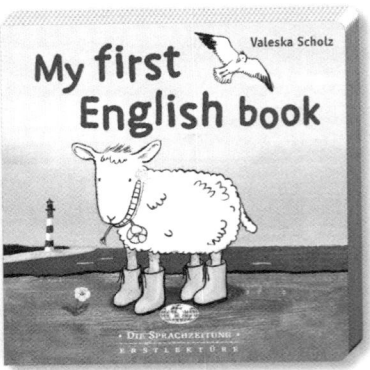